Good Customer Service Tips for Entrepreneurs

Please & Thank You with a Smile

Table of Contents

Thank you for purchasing this book!

In it I hope that you find some peace of mind and skills on how to deal with your customers and employees to foster a wonderful workplace environment as well as being a part of making a customer satisfied with a smile.

A little about why I did this book:

I have worked with the public for over 20 years in various industries. I've worked in restaurants, front offices, corner grocery stores, day cares and even ministries. And I've dealt with all types of people. And one thing I've learned is that everyone wants to be treated with respect. But sometimes people don't know how to give it or go about getting it.

In this book, I hope that you learn from my mistakes, and also take the wisdom I am giving to grow as a person and as a professional. Customer Service is one the biggest issues with all businesses (and ministries) today. I truly believe if businesses had better customer service practices, sales would skyrocket and employee turnover rates would drop tremendously. So, as you read, evaluate yourself and take whatever nuggets that I've shared to apply it to you becoming more successful and happy with who you are and where you're going.

Successfully Yours,

Tonya

Why Is Customer Service Important?

First, let's see what customer service is. It is defined as the assistance and advice provided by a company to those people who buy or use its products or services.[1]

Let's break that down a little more. It is when you help people in how to buy your products or use your services. You are a representative of who your company is, why it's important to your customers, and how it helps your customers. This is an important definition to remember, because many believe customer service is just a complaint station. But when you as the provider understands what customer service actually is, you can better help your customer.

Customer service is important in making sure that your representation of your company is presented in the best possible light and the image of your business produces an attractive brand... Sounds confusing, I know. Okay, check this: Say for instance you sell handbags. The image you want to present to people is that your handbags are of good quality, they are attractive, they are convenient in the size, and they are cost-efficient. Now, you have a customer who purchased one of your handbags, and two weeks after she bought it, the shoulder strap breaks. Your image that you sell good quality handbags is damaged. How important do you think it is to restore that image to your current customer and future customers? Very important, right? That's why customer service is crucial. It restores and sustains your image to your customer base so that they are happy, return customers and also refer new customers. In the end, you make money and keep making money while making people happy. Sounds good, huh? But is it as easy as it sounds? We will find out in the sections ahead.

---

[1] Google.com

Who Does Customer Service Apply To?

When you hear the words customer service, you automatically think about angry or complaining customers. But all customers need customer service. Remember our definition? The point of customer service is to give assistance in how a customer uses a service or buys a product.

Your best customers even need help. They need to *feel appreciated* for spending their money with you, *feel comfortable* in trusting you with their needs, and *feel valued* to be a part of your business. All of these points are necessary to fulfill in providing great customer service to your customers.

But there is also another sector that customer service applies to - your employees. If you are a business owner or manager reading this, this section is especially designed for you.

I know you're probably rolling your eyes or getting ready to flip to the next section, but wait! This section is just as important to your revenue... I hope I have your attention now.

See, employees are your representatives. They are the face to your products and services. They are an immediate part of your brand. So, it behooves you to take stock into this section.

I want to provide some stats right quick. Taking a look at one of the biggest employee turnover industries: hospitality, the top three causes for quitting their jobs are:
- Lack of advancement
- Poor working conditions
- Temporary work assignments[2]

The biggest reason mentioned on why employees quit is due to lack of appreciation and recognition. Hmm, sounds like our customers, doesn't it? Remember that our customers want to feel appreciated, comfortable in trusting you, and valued. Those same principles apply to your employees. Look at it like this: they are your first customers. You have to "sell" the job to them, and once you "sell" it to them, you have to service them to keep them coming (to work).

Employees that feel appreciated, comfortable in trusting you, and valued by you will learn how to appreciate and value your customers and make them comfortable in trusting them. This customer service thing is a reciprocal thing. Seeing your employees in the manner as being what I like to call your "first base" customers will show a transformation in your business.

There are various ways that you can provide customer service to your employees such as:
- providing adequate work hours
- making the environment comfortable, yet professional
- host appreciation week gifts or goodies
- send regular thank-you's to employees on meeting company goals
- provide bonuses

The ideas I listed above are good ways to build good customer service with your employees, but also establish a relationship with your employees. These are the people that represent you and your company, and you are a team. Be conscious that they are people too, and they have needs and concerns. Allow your employees to have input in team-building decisions, have an open-door policy for employees to come and express their concerns in a professional manner, and celebrate achievements with your employees. This builds morale and shows your employees that you value them.

Another sector that customer service applies to is vendors and supporters. These are the people that supply for you to meet your demand. Vendors are the least likely to get bad customer service, but there are instances when vendors experience it. Even if you never thought about vendors and customer service, it is important that you provide good service to your vendors.

Supporters are usually the people that hold that funds to support your special events, programs, incentives, and other stuff. Good customer service doesn't mean that you're sucking up to them, but you are showing that you value them, that what they provide for you is appreciated, and you have built a rapport that makes them comfortable to support you and your business. In the sections ahead, I have some ideas that I have for appreciating employees, but it works well with vendors and supporters as well. Remember this, a little bit goes a long way when you're sincere and on purpose with what you do.

Knowing Your Role

You're a boss, right? You're the one calling the shots, and you make things happen. Yep, that sounds about right. On your job description when you were hired, this is what you were told you were to do... or was that how you interpreted it?

It's key to understand your role in the success of your company or business. I know you're wondering what the heck does this have to do with customer service, huh? Well, it plays a big role. If you understand what you're supposed to do, then you will understand how to service your customers.

As the "boss" you're not just the big cheese that dictates orders and observes that they get done. You are the host. You are the one who showcases your products or services to your customers. Do you remember Barker's Beauties on the Price is Right? How they smiled and showcased the items to entice them to bid?

Well, that's sort of what you do. Your role as a representative is important in displaying the product or service and why the customer needs it.

Evaluate if you as the boss know the ins and outs of your products and services. I've encountered in my experience many supervisors who had no idea how a product worked or the intricate features of it. They just supervised that we knew and made sure we sold it. They didn't have a personal stake in what they were in charge of, and it affected our sales. If a customer complained, they only offered their book knowledge on the product, and when that didn't satisfy the customer, they ended up giving more than they got in return from them.

What I mean is this: if you really know your product and/or service, and you know your customer, when problems arise, you are able to appeal to the reason why they bought it, and what you can do to remind them of their need for it, and dissolve the negatives by amplifying the positives because of one simple thing – you know the product.

Your role as the boss – or even the employee – is not just to "sell," it is to serve the customer's needs.

It's More Than a Job

Working in customer service can be a strenuous job. It can be taxing, and feel like you're the dumping post for your customers. That's what customer service has been "reduced" to. It has been considered as a menial job that no one wants, but each business knows is necessary.

I'd like to twist the mentality of what customer service is, and the value of the position. So far, in the previous sections, I think I've been able to establish the foundation of why customer service is important. But I want to change the mindset of how it is viewed.

Being a customer service representative is more than just a job. It is an important line of defense in selling your product or service. Shift your mindset to a secret service op. As an agent, you have to know your assignment. You have to know what their weaknesses are, what your mission is, and be top-notch in using the skills to accomplish your mission.

This is sort of the mindset you have to take. You are not just doing a job. You're an important part of building customers and growing the company. Build your customer service based on necessity. Remember I said earlier the points of a customer wanting to purchase from you? When you understand that this is not just a job you're doing, you will be more of a value to your customers.

As an employer or supervisor, knowing how important each facet of your business will yield in great success. From the customer service representative to the top executive, each plays an important part in the success of your business.

Change your mentality from insignificant to significant! The more you care about a product or service, the more someone will want to buy it from you. We'll talk more about this in the next section.

Having the Right Frame of Mind

I've alluded to this topic in the past two sections, but we're going to really get in-depth with your mindset.

How you think is key to how you work. So a man thinks, so he is. And what that means is that your thoughts dictate your actions. Having the right mindset will yield having the right attitude.

Have you ever wondered how when your mad at the world, you come to work, you tend to get all of the angry customers? That's because you've attracted the same attitudes that you have.

Sounds crazy, but it's true. It's not to say that because you have a bad attitude all of the negative people are just going to gravitate toward you, but you tend to get what you give.

That's why it's important to know what your role is and why customer service is important. If you don't have these two concepts down, you're in for a struggle in keeping your customers happy.

Now, that's part of your mindset. You should strive to make your customers happy. If you have happy customers, you make more money. Your customers tell other people who can be your potential new customers, and if your current customers have bad experiences with you, they will warn others.

Don't think that your product supersedes everything. Good quality customer service is the packaging of your product or service. Attract customers to your products or services, and keep them engaged and if there is a problem that arises, look to solve the problem more than getting them to keep your product or service.

In your mind, you have to be hospitality-minded. I recall when I first started working at a restaurant. I had the mind that the restaurant guests were there for me to make a paycheck. They came to eat, they left a tip, and I got the money. My attitude was not of service. I didn't always have a pleasant demeanor because I didn't think about being hospitable; I just thought about doing the job. And I wondered why my customers didn't tip me as well as some of the others.

I had to change my mindset. I had to be the June Cleaver of waitressing. It no longer had to be about me and what I wanted out of the deal. I had a service to perform, products to promote, and I had to learn the needs of my customers and how the products would fulfill those needs.

Your mindset should always be about the customer. I know it seems sucky that you are putting yourself on the back-burner, but in reality, you are putting your money on the front-burner. If people don't buy your products or services, you don't make any money anyway. And the best kind of marketing is you!

Market yourself, be the most hospitable person you've ever seen, and watch the change in your business.

Ponder this:

You are a consumer. You are eyeing a nice jewelry set at a jewelry store. The clerk smiles and as you continue to peruse the showcase, you find the item you want to purchase. The clerk gets busy with another customer, but glances at you while you get his attention with eye contact. The clerk continues to speak with the other customer, and shares a couple of laughs. You check your watch and realize you've been standing and waiting for almost fifteen minutes since the clerk looked in your direction. You're getting antsy and are ready to leave the store because you feel you're being ignored and the clerk must not want to sell you the jewelry.

Now look at this:

You are the clerk. You watch a potential customer taking their time looking at the jewelry cases of the store. You smile at him, and get edgy that he's been in the store for twenty minutes already, and hasn't made a move to purchase. Your attention is captured by a new customer that comes in and seems to automatically know what they want. You see a definite sale. You hone in and give your greatest presentation. From your peripheral view, you see the first customer standing at one of the cases. He looks like he might be ready to purchase, but you definitely got your eye fixed on this customer in front of you. Your focus is on making what looks like a big sale, that you almost forget the first customer.

Can you see how the first scenario, you as the consumer would be agitated with the service you received from the clerk? And in the second scenario, how you as the clerk had the wrong type of mindset? You as the clerk must have the mindset of the customer. What I mean is that however you would want to be treated as a customer, is the way you as a customer service representative treat your customers.
Put yourself in the shoes of your customers. Think about what you need as a customer, and give that to your own customers. Change the way you think. It's not about the sale, but the value of the sell.

Steps to Handling the Angry Customer

This section will include some of my personal testimonies in how I dealt with angry customers in the right and wrong way. I hope in this section that if you learn nothing else, you learn how to handle yourself properly when situations like this arise. Remember, these steps apply to internal as well as external customers.

In handling angry customers, you have to understand why they're angry. And I want to make it clear that you're not going to make everyone happy. Some people are going to be angry no matter what you do to please them, but the key is to do all you possibly can to fix the problem, and restore the trust in you and your product or service.

I remember when Hurricane Katrina hit, and we had an influx of restaurant guests come in to eat. I had one guest who said I gave her a dirty glass. Now, it was my fault that I didn't double-check the glass to make sure the dishwashers had washed it thoroughly before I served it. I quickly grabbed the glass and replaced it with a fresh glass of water. Next, she complained that the water was not cold enough. She asked for a glass of ice. I brought the ice, and guess what, she never drunk the glass of water. Two weeks later, I received a write-up from the home office stating that I was rude and never brought her a glass of water. But there was three glasses of water on her table – that she never drank.

Here is what I learned from that lesson. I didn't assess her situation. I was looking at the sale, instead of the value of the sell. This woman more than likely had been through a great ordeal, being misplaced by such a tragic storm and all I did was drop off glass after glass of water as if she was pestering me – which truthfully, she was. But I lacked good customer service. I justified that I brought what she asked for, but I missed the value!

I have an event consulting business, and in my training manual for staff I list ways on how to treat our clients and their guests when we are hired. I'd like to share some of those tips here, because it has really been a help to me in developing better customer relations with my clients.

1. **Listen** to your customer. Listen to what they are complaining about, and also here's something a little tricky: listen to what they are NOT saying. Many times, people lash out in anger because they're upset about something else, have had a bad experience with a prior

representative, overwhelmed or are under the influence. Pay attention to "clue" reasons on why they're REALLY angry. Listen to them, and do not be so quick to interrupt or "correct" them. Hear them out to gather as much information as possible. When people are angry, they usually "let it all hang out."

2. **Restate the problem back to the customer**. This expresses to the customer that you are listening to them, and concerned about getting the issue resolved.

3. **Sympathize with the customer**. Remember your customer wants to feel comfortable with trusting you with their needs. Having rules and regulations in place are indeed important, but present it to them with clarity and empathy for their dissatisfaction. Offer solutions that will encourage your customer's trust in not only your knowledge about the product or service, but also your ability to help them at all cost. This is good customer service!

4. **Be objective**. Provide solutions that will not just meet your needs or to pacify your customers. You want to meet company regulations, and provide the best service to your customers. Recall your policies, but not in a patronizing manner; re-educate your customer on why your policies are in place and how they are there to protect and help them. Integrity is very important. Your customers don't want to feel that you will tell them anything just to make them feel good, but find out it's a lie that is more harm than helping them. Use common sense, and remember that how you would want someone to treat you in the situation, you should use those same principles of courtesy.

5. **Handle matters quickly**. Don't let a situation go on without getting it handled. The longer you allow a situation remain unresolved and a customer is unsatisfied, the longer the customer has to be controlled by their emotions. Emotional situations are irrational situations. Allowing a situation to be unresolved does serious damage to your customer's belief that you value them as customers. If you are unable to resolve it yourself, immediately involve a supervisor or someone who can fix it; just don't let it fall by the wayside.

In the past, I've made so many mistakes myself by allowing situations to go unresolved, or just doing what was "policy" to get rid of a customer. It may have resolved the situation at that time, but it left a mark on the image of the company that I worked for. Just little ole me had a great impact on whether that customer would frequent us again or hinder new ones to come.

Remember your role, and how important you are in building your business. Customer service is key to making and keeping money, so make sure you understand that how you problem-solve is also instrumental – even crucial to building or hurting your reputation and relationship with your customers.

Professional Courtesy to Employees

I know I touched on this a little bit earlier, but it bears digging a little more into in this section. As an employer, your main goal is to make money, right?

No, your main goal is foster the operations of maintaining a successful business that helps meet a need for consumers. Once you understand that, you will know how to treat your employees as a business owner or supervisor.

I stated some ways to express good customer service to your employees in an earlier chapter. Now I want to share with you how to express professional courtesy. The two are similar, but they aren't exactly the same. Let me share this:

My Experience Reflection
I served as an office manager, and I had an employee that was often late for work. She had different excuses as to why she was late. Once her boyfriend called in for her and said she was sick. She didn't show up the next day – even after I called to see if she was coming to work (Yes I did call. I know, don't gasp). Now, I could have just written her pink slip and put it in her paycheck envelope. I would have been well within my right to do so, but I realized that my employees were people, too. How many times have I been late due to some unforeseen situation? Sometimes we just have a bad week.

Professional courtesy includes putting yourself in someone else's shoes. It is not, I repeat, it is not a license to let employees get away with doing whatever they want. But what it is, is establishing and fostering the value of your employees in your company.

supervised customer service reps (go figure) as well as receptionist and other office staff. And normally, people believe CSRs are expendable and they come a dime a dozen. And the truth is, they do. But if you want to build a valuable relationship with your customers, you have to start with building that same relationship with your employees. Think of your employees as your first line of customers (remember I called them "first base" earlier?). Once you've managed to accomplish first base, then you can move to second base to build customers, and third base to get referrals.

Other ways to express professional courtesy to your employees is to build their self-esteem in your company. This is another value nugget. If your employees know they are valued, and important to your company, believe me, their work ethic will change immensely and their interaction with your customers will be awesome.
And don't be afraid to share some of your awesome sauce with your employees. I'm not saying give away the company secrets, but share with them the opportunities to move up in the company, and train them to be better at their jobs. This is what I call investment. It is important that your employees feel that you care about how well they do their jobs, and how their jobs affect their personal lives as well. If your employees see that you view their job as important, they will see it as important. Are we getting the picture?

I know I'm presenting something very challenging, because not many people consider this as the norm. But I have a prime example of this:

My Experience Reflection
As an office manager, I had an employee that I viewed with potential. I "created" a position to give her an incentive to work harder and not see her role with our company as insignificant or disposable. I gave her extra tasks to sharpen her skills and to

prepare her for the next level. Her work ethic began to skyrocket! Her competitiveness kicked in high gear, and she started actually evaluating herself against the other CSRs on how many calls she made per week. She actually took stock in how the numbers stacked up at the end of the week, and what those results meant for the company at-large.

I know that this seems worthless, but believe me, when you view your employees as customers, you begin to see a greater value in your buying customers. It's a very common business practice, but not many upper management use it because of fear and not knowing how to put these practices into use properly.

Believe me when I tell you this, you won't lose your authority when you follow these principles. If anything, you will gain even more respect, and your employees will be more engaging and more apt to be honest and get on board with the vision and goals of your business.

Wooing Referrals

This is the stage that you want to achieve with good customer service. You want your customers to keep coming back, and bring others along with them.

One thing I've learned is that you can exhaust your existing customers, which will cause them to lose interest in your product or services. Change things up and provide incentive. Market your incentives for building referrals in a way where they are not thinking that you're only offering the incentive just to get their referrals.

When I worked for an insurance company, one of the things that was stressed to the agents was building referrals. I had to provide ways to share with our agents on how to build persistency – in other words, keep them paying. Offering the ideas of the product was good, but guess what, others offered the same products. But to build referrals you have to move a step further. I'd like to share some ideas for you to toss around.

Let me make this clear, there is no magic answer to building referrals. Everything is really trial and error. You know your target audience (customers) and what they need, and what they want. Appeal to their wants by addressing their needs first. Wants are transient and change quickly. But needs are consistent UNTIL they are met. Society gravitates to what's popular, but they will always have needs, and that's what you as a business owner, manager, or employee want to address at all times as your first priority.

Good customer service doesn't mean that you're giving away the store, but it means you are doing your best to help meet your customers' needs and keep them satisfied. Referrals come because they've "heard" about how you treated someone else. Understand who referrals are. They are potential new customers that have the similar needs as your existing customers. The difference between a new customer and a referral is that referrals already have pre-conceived ideas about you and your business. They are coming aboard based on someone else's experience.

In building referrals, try this: offer discounts, or special privileges for return customers. Also keep the communication lines open and active with your customers. This builds on those trust and value factors. Customers are more likely to refer someone to you if they see that you care about their NEEDS and not just about their money.

Making the Most Out of Good Customer Service

Good customer service is what you make it to be. A changed mindset and a desire to improve your business is key in establishing it.

Customer service is necessary to grow your business and make it stand out among other businesses in your niche. People will always want to spend money, but a good reputation will be what makes your business stellar and your money make money for you.

I really have learned a lot of things about customer service in the 20-plus years that I've been in the workforce. I've seen businesses shut down simply because bad customer service with employees provided a domino effect to loss of external or second-base customers. I have even listened to other business owners complain about not patronizing other businesses because of bad customer service.

Businesses can succeed without a good customer service plan in place, but they struggle to make it, have high turnovers, consistent policy changes, and so much more than they really should. Along with policy implementation, dress code as well as many factors, customer service is right at the top of being an important factor in building a successful company or business.

To make the most out of it, re-evaluate your vision and make sure that your employees are aware of it. Make them apart of the vision and encourage your employees to manifest it daily in their interaction with your external customers.

Teach yourself how to be a team player – even as management. Customer service is about teamwork. No one man or woman can build a business. It takes a team to know the vision and implement the vision. High morale among your employees begins with management. Management has to set the tone for the atmosphere for the company. Remember, your employees will only do what they see you do and what you allow them to do. If you don't respect them, they will less likely respect your customers. Honor your hierarchy not as a way to divide your team, but as a way to motivate your team. Be the type of management that your employees can appreciate, trust and value.

Don't just dress and write the part, but be the part. Be the solution that you plan to be for your second and third base customers. The best way to woo your customers is show how you exemplify it with your employees. Have such a great customer service plan in place with your employees that they will become instant and *genuine* testimonials to your customers.

Just Try It!

This section is a list of simulations that you can use in your workplace to train your managers on customer service. They are most commonly chance mock situations, with questions at the end.

Remember to keep the 3 top needs of your 3 types of customers in mind as you answer your questions and address these situations.

First Base Customer: The Disgruntled Employee

Maxine has worked for the XYZ Company for almost a year. She has missed only one day of work due to a sick child all year long, and has even come in on weekends and holidays when asked. Her production numbers have improved the company's ratings and profits in nearly six months. At today's production meeting, she left a little angry, and has now come into your office to speak with you. You have been Maxine's supervisor ever since she started working for the company. Although the profits have increased, your company has additional expenses that have to be addressed. You think Maxine is a good employee, but she tends to get snippy with co-workers and some of your clients while she's on the phone with them when she's under a lot of pressure. She has expressed the following list of complaints. What do you do? And why?

Maxine's complaints:

- Haven't had a pay raise since her 90-day probation
- Continues to work in a small cubby she shares with two other employees that's drafty and smells
- Has only one bathroom break an hour
- Her department was not given any credit for the new profits that they stayed up working for hours on to produce

YOUR PLAN OF ACTION –

1. How to show appreciation:
2. How to gain trust:
3. How to show her you value her:
4. Your attitude toward her complaints:
5. Your attitude toward her weaknesses:

Second Base Customer: The Frustrated Customer

Lyle purchased some equipment from your company XYZ. He has purchased from you before, and you've never had a complaint from him. He purchased the equipment three months ago, and has called you – the employee – screaming about how the parts were rusted and only worked for him once. He goes into a rant about threatening to write a negative review to your corporate office, and how he wasted his last $40 on such a sorry piece of equipment. He wants a refund, although it's stated that the refund policy is active for only 60 days after purchase, and he used a coupon and there are no refunds on discounted items. What do you do? And why?

Lyle's customer profile:

- Has been a loyal customer for the last three years
- Has never had a complaint before
- Waited 90 days before reporting the problem
- Threatens to write to corporate office on the faulty equipment
- Says he spent his last $40 on the equipment, which he purchased at a discount

Thought Questions:

A. How do you think a negative review will impact your company? Your paycheck?

B. What "clues" did you pick up on in his conversation that will help you assess his "real" problem?

YOUR PLAN OF ACTION –

1. How to show appreciation:
2. How to gain trust:
3. How to show him you value him:
4. Your attitude toward his complaints:
5. Your attitude toward his weaknesses:

Third Base Customer: The Cynical Referral

Preston was referred to you by his long-time friend, Alice to purchase cable services. She informed him that she has been with XYZ Cable for almost ten years, and has not had any problems with her service. Preston has also heard from other customers that they don't get what they pay for, and the rates will increase dramatically after the first bill. You, as the customer service representative, are making calls to potential customers about a holiday special. Preston is one of the people on your list to call. As you give your scripted spiel, he cuts you off with the list of questions. What do you do? And why?

Preston's concerns and questions:

- I heard that people don't get the 40-channels for only $10 with a new customer full package?
- This is a rip-off. Why do y'all jack up the price after the first bill?
- How long is this special? What will my bill be next month?
- I heard this company has a lot of reception and satellite problems in this area

Your script/information:

"Hi valued friend. We at XYZ are offering a 90-day holiday special of 20 premier channels for only $29.99. We would love for you to try this offer out, and if you are satisfied after your trial period, we will take $10 off of your cable bill for the next two months."

- XYZ has the top-rated cable services in the tri-state area.
- Customer Care is available 24/7
- All first-time customers receive a 10% discount
- Your company's customer complaint ratio is 1 in 9
- Preston is new to the area, and needs internet and cable for his new job as a film critic college professor

YOUR PLAN OF ACTION –

1. How to show appreciation:
2. How to gain trust:
3. How to show him you value him:
4. Your attitude toward his concerns:
5. Your attitude toward his needs:

NOTES:

NOTES:

NOTES:

NOTES:

NOTES:

NOTES:

NOTES:

NOTES:

About the Author:

Tonya has been writing since the age of 13, and has had a love for words ever since. She serves as a contributing writer for various e-zine publications, and although she has written numerous books, this is her first professional work launched to the public. She is currently working on two other writings for small businesses as well as a non-fiction book for publication.

She is the Chief Administrative Officer/Owner of UpWrite Solutions, LLC that offers virtual services in marketing, event consulting, and basic office administration. She is a native Mississippian, but has lived abroad in Europe. She has a love for food, teaching, and reading.

Website: www.upwritesolutions.com
Facebook: www.facebook.com/upwritesolutions7
Instagram: www.instagram.com/upwritesolutions
Twitter: www.twitter.com/writeitright7
LinkedIn: www.linkedin.com/in/upwritesolutionsllc7
Pinterest: www.pinterest.com/upwritesolutions
Blog: www.blogspot.com/primeeventschatterbox
Tumblr: www.upwritesolutions.tumblr
YouTube: www.youtube.com/upwritesolutions